Experiencing Chinese

体验汉语

国际语言研究与发展中心

学生用书
初中
Student Book
Middle School
1 A

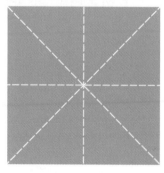

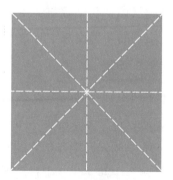
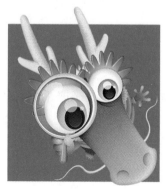
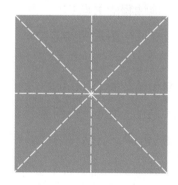

高等教育出版社
Higher Education Press

Printed in China

前　言

新学期开始了，欢迎一起来"体验汉语、体验快乐、体验成功"！

《体验汉语》初中系列教材是在中国国家汉语国际推广领导小组办公室（简称汉办）的合作与帮助下，由"国际语言研究与发展中心"专门为北美初中学生编写的系列汉语教材。

适用对象

本系列教材为零起点初中学生编写，适用对象为公立与私立中学 7—9 年级选修汉语课的学生，或 13—15 岁的汉语学习者，也可用于其他相应水平的汉语教学。

设计思想

本系列教材提倡体验式教学方法，力求创造快乐的学习氛围；选材贴近学生真实生活，旨在培养学习者的实用交际能力。

为了实现这些目标，编者在研究国际上英语等语言作为第二语言教学的教材基础上，汲取了汉语教材设计的成功经验，融合任务式、活动型教材设计方法，并本着本地化定制的原则，遵循外语教学大纲的"交际、文化、触类旁通、文化比较和社区"五个 C（Communication, Culture, Connection, Comparison and Community）原则，针对中学生汉语学习的条件和特点，在话题、功能、语法、课文内容和练习形式等方面进行了有益的尝试。

教材构成

本系列教材包括学生用书、练习册和教师用书，并配以 MP3 光盘和其他多媒体教学资源。本书为《体验汉语》初中教材学生用书第 1 册，由"学发音"和"学汉字"等 10 课构成，并附有两个复习课。本书的参考授课学时为 50 学时。

编写特色

本书具有以下编写特点：

■ 通过各种方式降低学习难度，激发学生的学习兴趣；

■ 听说领先，培养学生的实用交际能力；

■ 融合中西文化，促进跨文化沟通与理解；

■ 触类旁通，建立汉语能力与其他课程的关联；

■ 重视培养学生学以致用、融入社区生活需要的能力。

（一）话题

为了使教材的内容贴近学生真实生活，符合北美少年的学习和心理特征，采取了话题领先、结构配合的编写方式。以"我"为中心、由近及远，逐渐展开：从"我自己"到"我"的家庭、班级、学校，乃至社区、国家和世界等更大的范围，与结构结合形成每课的课文。

（二）课文

围绕一个关键句式，多故事、多画面重现；有的课文则在此基础上，更采取了同一个故事、同一个句型结构用多个画面重现的方法。同时，课文对话短小、精练、典型，便于学生朗读和背诵；情节幽默，尽量使学生体验到汉语学习的乐趣；文化对比蕴含于课文中，使学生在学习过程中逐渐加深对中国文化的了解。

（三）词汇与汉字

每课的基本生词控制在 10 个左右。在"语言放大镜"环节提供 4 个左右的扩展词汇，教师可根据学生情况灵活处理。每课的扩展词汇在下一册课本里，原则上将作为基本词汇复现。汉字书写与认读分流，由易到难，让学生循序渐进地掌握汉字书写的规律。

（四）语法

重视句式与结构的复现和训练，但在学生用书中不直接介绍语法知识，在教师用书里列出语法点的必要解释和讲练建议，由教师根据情况灵活处理。

（五）活动

每课的教学活动包括热身、会话、听力、口语、语音、汉字、文化和社区等。活动形式有两人活动、小组活动、全班活动、角色扮演、小调查和小制作等。其中，社区活动则是本教材的一个重要环节，旨在训练学习者在真实生活环境中运用汉语的能力。

（六）文化

"体验中国"部分用英、汉双语提供了简单有趣的中国文化知识，以加强学生对中国的了解，为进一步的跨文化沟通与交际打下基础。

（七）版式

该系列教材的封面和正文版式均融合了中西方的元素，生动活泼，图文并茂，总体风格现代而富有少年趣味，采用了绘图、图片、照片等形式，使内容更加真实、生动。

鸣　谢

感谢中国教育部国际合作司和中国国家汉办给予的大力支持和指导。感谢 Harry Gao 先生对本系列教材所做的英语审订工作。

最后，我们愿以这套教材与汉语学习者分享学习汉语的快乐，祝愿你们获得更丰富的体验、更成功的人生！

国际语言研究与发展中心

2008 年 5 月

Contents

Topic	Text	Function	Main sentence structu
1 My name **25**	你好! Hello!	Greeting Say goodbye Self-introduction	我是飞飞。 我姓王，叫王飞飞。
2 My friend **33**	你真好! It's very nice of you!	Praise Express one's thanks	你真好!
3 Numbers and fruits **41**	五个香蕉 Five bananas	Put forward request Express quantity	我要五个香蕉。
4 My favorite animals **49**	我喜欢狗 I like dogs	Express your favorite	我喜欢狗。

Topic	Text	Function	Main sentence structu
5 My appearance **59**	我的眼睛很大 I have big eyes	Describe appea-rance	我的眼睛很大。
6 My family **67**	这是我妈妈 This is my mother	Introduction	这是我妈妈。
7 My room **75**	看，我的电脑 Look, my computer	Describe the posi-tion of an object	电脑在桌子的上边。
8 My school (stationery) **83**	这不是你的书包 This is not your bag	Apologize and res-pond to apologies Express negation	这不是你的书包。

| Tones | Finals | Initials | Syllables |
| Strokes | Structures | Writing orders | |

Grammar	Phonetics	Chinese characters	Culture	Community activities
Sentences with 是 Special question with 什么	a o e i u ü	十 八	Chinese family names	Make large cards of Chinese names
Adjective predicate sentence with the adverb 真 们 expresses plural	ai ei ao ou	人 丁	56 nationalities	Make a poster of your favorite celebrity in Chinese
二 and 两 quantifiers as attributes Special question with 呢	an en in ang eng ing ong	土 木	Chinese cities	Draw a picture of your favorite fruit
Third person pronoun 也 as an adverb Right and wrong question with 吗	ie ia ua uo üe	上 下	12 animals of the Chinese Zodiac	Observe and get to know the Chinese names of people's pets
Adjective predicate sentence with the adverb 很 的 as a structural particle	j q x	大 口	the Great Wall	Create a "perfect face" with the most charming facial features of different celebrities
这 and 那 demonstrative pronouns Pronoun taken as an attribute Special question with 谁	zh ch sh r	工 王	Confucius	Make your family tree in Chinese
Sentences with 在 expressing position Special question with 哪儿	z c s	日 月	the Yangtze River and the Yellow River	Draw or take a picture of your desk to introduce your objects to your classmates
Negative sentence with 不	z-zh c-ch s-sh	山 小	Chinese kungfu	Make a list of your personal objects

目 录

话 题		课 文	功 能	主要句型
1	我的姓名 25	你好!	打招呼 告别 自我介绍	我是飞飞。 我姓王，叫王飞飞。
2	我的朋友 33	你真好!	赞美 道谢	你真好!
3	数字与水果 41	五个香蕉	提出要求 表达数量	我要五个香蕉。
4	我喜欢的动物 49	我喜欢狗	表达喜好	我喜欢狗。
	复习课 **1** 57			
5	我的相貌 59	我的眼睛很大	描述相貌	我的眼睛很大。
6	我的家人 67	这是我妈妈	介绍	这是我妈妈。
7	我的房间 75	看，我的电脑	描述物品的 位置	电脑在桌子的上边。
8	我的学校 （学习用品） 83	这不是你的书包	道歉与回应 否定	这不是你的书包。

汉语的声调　汉语的韵母　汉语的声母　汉语的音节
汉字的笔画　汉字的结构　汉字的书写顺序

语　法	语　音	认写汉字	文　化	社区活动
"是"字句 用"什么"的特殊疑问句	a o e i u ü	十　八	中国人的姓氏	制作中文名字大卡片
使用副词"真"的形容词谓语句 "们"表示复数	ai ei ao ou	人　丁	56个民族	用汉语制作喜欢的明星的招贴画
数量词作定语 "二"和"两" 用"呢"的特殊疑问句	an en in ang eng ing ong	土　木	中国的城市	用汉语制作喜欢的水果的图片
第三人称代词 副词"也" 用"吗"的是非疑问句	ie ia ua uo üe	上　下	中国的12生肖	观察并了解周围宠物的汉语名称和名字
使用副词"很"的形容词谓语句 结构助词"的"	j q x	大　口	长城	用各种明星最有魅力的五官打造一个"完美形象"
指示代词"这"和"那" 代词作定语 用"谁"的特殊疑问句	zh ch sh r	工　王	孔子	用汉语做一个自己家庭的大树图
"在"字句表位置 用"哪儿"的特殊疑问句	z c s	日　月	长江与黄河	描画或拍摄自己的书桌向同学介绍自己的物品
用"不"的否定句	z-zh c-ch s-sh	山　小	中国功夫	做一张自己个人物品的统计表

课堂用语

Expressions for Classroom

Class begins.
现在开始上课。 Xiànzài kāishǐ shàng kè.

Please turn to page X.
请翻到第X页。 Qǐng fān dào dì X yè.

Read after me.
跟我读。 Gēn wǒ dú.

Do not look at the textbook, and read after me.
不看书，跟我读。 Bú kàn shū, gēn wǒ dú.

(Read it) Together.
一起(读)。 Yìqǐ (dú).

Please repeat.
请重复一遍。 Qǐng chóngfù yí biàn.

Please look at the new words.
请看生词。 Qǐng kàn shēngcí.

Please look at the exercises.
请看练习。 Qǐng kàn liànxí.

Please pair up and do the dialogue exercises.
两人一组，做对话练习。 Liǎng rén yì zǔ, zuò duìhuà liànxí.

Who can answer the question?
谁能回答这个问题？ Shuí néng huídá zhège wèntí?

Please answer the question.
请你回答。 Qǐng nǐ huídá.

Any questions?
有问题吗？ Yǒu wèntí ma?

Pay attention to the tones/intonation.
注意声调/语调。 Zhùyì shēngdiào/ yǔdiāo.

Next one.
下一个。 Xià yí gè.

Finished?
做完了吗？ Zuò wán le ma?

Please look at the blackboard.
请大家看黑板。 Qǐng dàjiā kàn hēibǎn.

Correct.
对。 Duì.

Incorrect.
不对。 Bú duì.

Very good.
很好。 Hěn hǎo.

Please listen to the recording.
请听录音。 Qǐng tīng lùyīn.

Clear?
听懂了吗？ Tīng dǒng le ma?

Please close your books.
请合上书。 Qǐng hé shàng shū.

Today's class will end now.
今天的课就上到这儿。 Jīntiān de kè jiù shàng dào zhèr.

Class is over.
下课。 Xià kè.

学发音
Learning Pronunciation

The Tones of Chinese 汉语的声调

In Chinese, there are four tones and one neutral tone that express different meanings and can be represented by four marks.

汉语普通话里有四个声调和一个轻声，它们能表示不同的意义，四个声调分别用四个声调符号来表示。

Recognize the Chinese tone marks.
认一认，汉语的声调符号。

Read.
读一读。

Listen and write down the tone marks.
听一听，写一写声调符号。

Draw flash cards and learn pronunciation.

抽卡片，学发音。

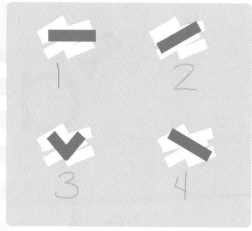

Play the "message-passing game".

玩一玩，做"传话游戏"。

There are six basic finals in Chinese.

汉语有六个基本韵母。

Read and write.

读一读，写一写。

Sing the Chinese final song.

唱一唱，汉语韵母歌。

a o e i u ü　a ā á ǎ à　o ō ó ǒ ò

e ē é ě è　i ī í ǐ ì　u ū ú ǔ ù　ü ǖ ǘ ǚ ǜ

a o e i u ü　tǐ yàn hàn yǔ hǎo kuài lè

Let's play "should you stand up"?

玩一玩，你是不是该站起来？

Read and recognize.

读一读，认一认。

ai	ao	an	ang
ou	ong		
ei	en	eng	er
iu	ie	ia	in	ing
ui	uo	ua	un
üe	ün		

Listen to the recording, and mark the tones you hear above the larger letter.

听录音，在比较大的字母上边标出你听到的声调。

ai ao an ang
ou ong
ei en eng er
iu ie ia in ing ui
uo ua un
üe ün

The Initials of Chinese 汉语的声母

Recognize the initials of Chinese.

认一认，汉语的声母。

b	p	m	f
d	t	n	l
g	k	h	
j	q	x	
zh	ch	sh	r
z	c	s	

Sing the Chinese initial song.

唱一唱，汉语声母歌。

a o e i u ü
b p m f d t n l
g k h j q x
zh ch zh r z c s
nǐ lái chàng
wǒ lái chàng
a o e de gē

Read and write.

读一读，写一写。

b　p　m　f　d　t　n　l

b　p　m　f　d　t　n　l

g　k　h　j　q　x

g　k　h　j　q　x

zh　ch　sh　r　z　c　s

zh　ch　sh　r　z　c　s

Listen and point in the order you hear.

听一听，按听到的顺序指一指。

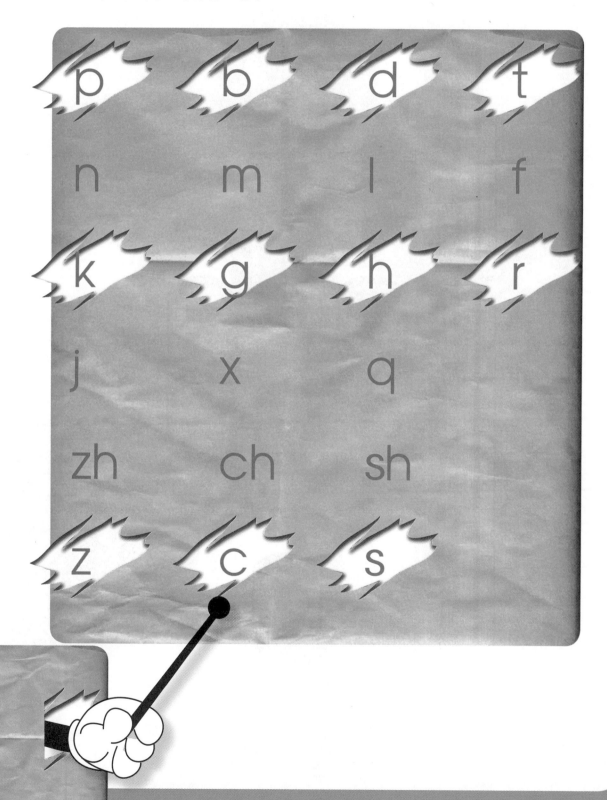

The Syllables of Chinese 汉语的音节

Look at the pictures and read.

看图片，读一读。

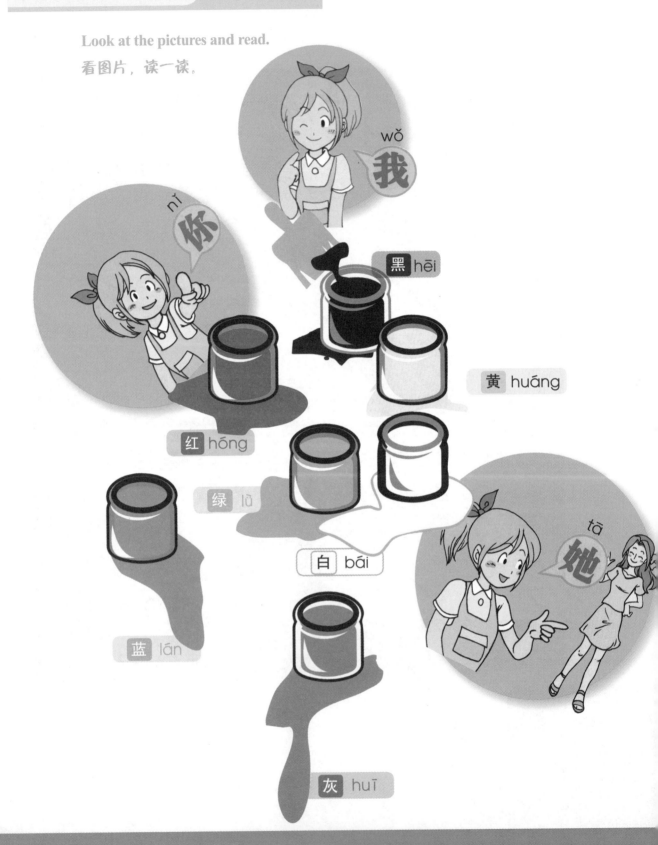

wǒ 我

nǐ 你

黑 hēi

黄 huáng

红 hóng

绿 lǜ

白 bái

tā 她

蓝 lán

灰 huī

Read.

读一读。

| nǐ hǎo | xiǎo niǎo | xiǎo gǒu | jǐ diǎn | hěn hǎo | hěn lěng |

yì tiān	yìzhí	yìqǐ	yíyàng
yìbiān	yì tóu	yì bǎ	yí gè
yìxiē	yì míng	yì kǒu	yíxià

bù gāo	bù cháng	bù hǎo	bú dà
bù chī	bù máng	bù xiǎo	bú shì
bù hē	bù liáng	bù měi	bú rè

māma	yéye	nǎinai	xièxie
gēge	tóufa	jiějie	bàba
zhuōzi	bízi	běnzi	dìdi
tāmen	shítou	nǐmen	mèimei

学汉字
Learning Chinese Characters

Seemingly complicated Chinese characters have only six basic strokes: the horizontal stroke, vertical stroke, left-falling stroke, right-falling stroke, lifting stroke and point stroke, from which other strokes are constructed.

看似复杂的汉字其实只有六种基本笔画，分别叫横（一）、竖（丨）、撇（丿）、捺（丶）、点（丶）、提（㇀），其他笔画都是由这六种笔画变化出来的。

Recognize the basic strokes of Chinese characters.

认一认，汉字的基本笔画。

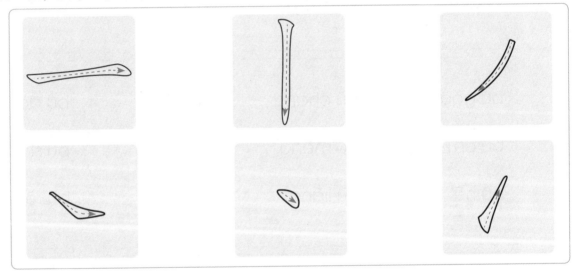

Which stroke is missing in each of the following characters? Please write out the missing stroke.

下面的汉字缺少哪一笔？请你补上。

bīng	rì	shān	bā	rén	xīn
冰	日	山	八	人	心

Learning Chinese Characters

Recognize and trace over: other strokes of Chinese characters.

认一认，描一描：汉字的其他笔画。

The Structures of Chinese Characters 汉字的结构

Recognize the single form and combined form of Chinese characters.

认一认，独体字和合体字。

wǒ	tóu	tiān
我	头	天

single form 独体字

guó	shuài	shì
国	帅	是

combined form 合体字

Recognize different combined forms of Chinese characters.

认一认，不同的合体字。

bà	hǎo	huí
爸	好	回

Circle the one character with a different structure in each line below.

下面每行字中都有一个字与其他字结构不同，试着把它圈出来。

tā	wǔ	yě	wǒ
她	五	也	我

mā	bà	jiě	shī
妈	爸	姐	师

gāo	guó	tài	shì
高	国	泰	是

shuài	hěn	yǎn	lǎo
帅	很	眼	老

The Writing Orders of Chinese Characters 汉字的书写顺序

Chinese people write character strokes in a particular order. In a reasonable order, characters can be written quickly and beautifully.

中国人书写汉字笔画是有先后顺序的，按照合理的顺序书写汉字，写出来的字又快又好看。

First top then bottom 先上后下	èr 二	一 → 二
First left then right 先左后右	hǎo 好	女 → 好
First left-falling stroke, then right-falling stroke 先撇后捺	rén 人	丿 → 人
First horizontal stroke, then vertical stroke 先横后竖	shí 十	一 → 十
First outside then inside 先外后里	fēng 风	几 → 风
First center then sides 先中间后两边	xiǎo 小	亅 → 小
First fill in then seal 先填中后封口	guó 国	冂 → 国 → 国

学数字
Learning Numbers

Read and recognize.
认一认，读一读。

one	two	three	four	five
1 一	2 二	3 三	4 四	5 五
yī	èr	sān	sì	wǔ

six	seven	eight	nine	ten
6 六	7 七	8 八	9 九	10 十
liù	qī	bā	jiǔ	shí

Pair work. One student makes a gesture of a number, and then the other pronounces it in Chinese.
两人一组，一个同学用手势表示出数字，另一个同学用汉语说出该数字。

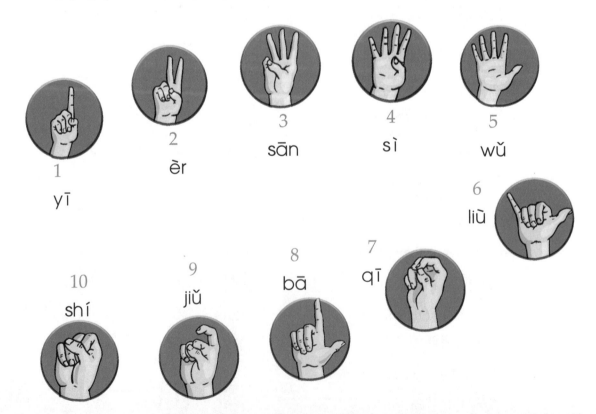

你 好！

第 1 课

Objectives 学习目标

⭕ **Learn to greet and say goodbye**
学会问候与告别

⭕ **Learn to introduce yourself**
学会介绍自己的姓名

Warm-up 热身

> 1　**Which countries' body languages for greetings do you know? Imitate them in front of your classmates.**
>
> 你知道哪些国家人们打招呼的身体语言？给同学们模仿一下吧。

> 2　**Check these commonly used Chinese given names. Which do you think are for girls and which are for boys?**
>
> 看一看中国人常用的名字，你觉得哪些是女孩儿常用的，哪些是男孩儿常用的？

伟	婷	龙	丽	海	芳	明
wěi	tíng	lóng	lì	hǎi	fāng	míng
great	slim	dragon	beautiful	ocean	fragrant	bright

娟	红	军	艳	玲	刚	峰
juān	hóng	jūn	yàn	líng	gāng	fēng
graceful	red	army	gorgeous	fairy	strong	apex

Conversation 会话

fēifei

你好! 我是飞飞。
Nǐ hǎo! Wǒ shì Fēifei.

你好，fēifei。
Nǐ hǎo, fēifei.

1

你好! 我是飞飞。
Nǐ hǎo! Wǒ shì Fēifei.

Fèifei，你好。
Fèifei, nǐ hǎo.

2

你好! 我是飞飞。
Nǐ hǎo! Wǒ shì Fēifei.

飞飞，你好。
Fēifei, nǐ hǎo.

3

再见，fèifei。
Zàijiàn, fèifei.

再见!
Zàijiàn!

4

Words
词语

你好 nǐ hǎo	我 wǒ	是 shì
hello	I, me	be (am, is, are)
什么 shénme	姓 xìng	
what	family name	

王飞飞：你好，我叫飞飞，你叫什么？
Wáng Fēifei:　Nǐ hǎo,　wǒ jiào Fēifei,　nǐ jiào shénme?

李明：我姓李，叫李明。飞飞，你姓什么？
Lǐ Míng:　Wǒ xìng Lǐ,　jiào Lǐ Míng.　Fēifei,　nǐ xìng shénme?

王飞飞：我姓王。
Wáng Fēifei:　Wǒ xìng Wáng.

 Language focus 语言放大镜

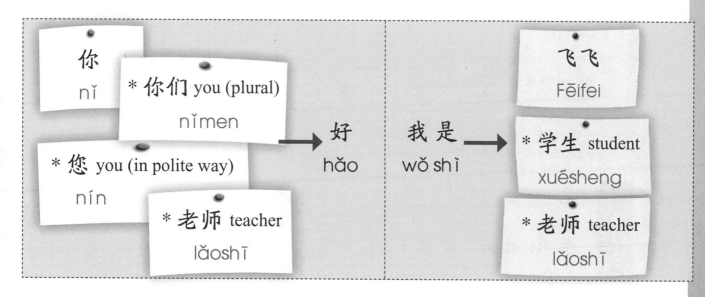

你
nǐ

* 你们 you (plural)
nǐmen

* 您 you (in polite way)
nín

* 老师 teacher
lǎoshī

→ 好
hǎo

我是 →
wǒ shì

飞飞
Fēifei

* 学生 student
xuésheng

* 老师 teacher
lǎoshī

再见 zàijiàn	叫 jiào	你 nǐ
goodbye	be called	you

王飞飞 Wáng Fēifei	李明 Lǐ Míng
Wang Feifei (a Chinese name)	Li Ming (a Chinese name)

Let's listen 听一听

1 Listen to the recording and match the pinyin to the words.

听录音，为词语选择拼音。

姓　叫　你好　再见　是　什么

zàijiàn　　nǐ hǎo　　shì　　shénme　　xìng　　jiào

Let's talk 说一说

1 Complete the following dialogues, and then use your own name to practice with your partner.

完成下面的对话，再用自己的名字与同伴练习。

1
王 飞飞：你好，_____。
Wáng Fēifei:　Nǐ hǎo,
李 明：你好，王 飞飞。
Lǐ Míng: Nǐ hǎo, Wáng Fēifei.

3
王 老师：你_____?
Wáng lǎoshī:　Nǐ
李 红：我 姓李，叫李红。
Lǐ Hóng: Wǒ xìng Lǐ,　jiào Lǐ Hóng.

2
李 明：你姓 什么?
Lǐ Míng:　Nǐ xìng shénme?
马丽：_____。
Mǎ Lì:

4
马丽：再见，张 红!
Mǎ Lì:　Zàijiàn, Zhāng Hóng!
张 红：_____!
Zhāng Hóng:

2   Listen to the recording and choose the sentences you hear.

听录音，选择你听到的句子。

1 你 好，飞 飞。 □   你 好，fēifei。 □
     Nǐ hǎo,   Fēifei.   Nǐ hǎo,   fēifei.

2 你 姓 什么？ □   你 叫 什么？ □
     Nǐ xìng shénme?   Nǐ jiào shénme?

3 飞飞 姓李。 □   飞飞 姓 王。 □
     Fēifei xìng Lǐ.   Fēifei xìng Wáng.

4 我 姓 李，叫李明。 □   我 姓 王，叫 王 明。 □
     Wǒ xìng Lǐ,   jiào Lǐ Míng.   Wǒ xìng Wáng, jiào Wáng Míng.

2   Close your eyes and guess who is talking.

蒙上眼睛，猜猜看，说话的人是谁？

Phonetics 语音

> 1 **Look, listen, and read.**
>
> 看一看，听一听，读一读。

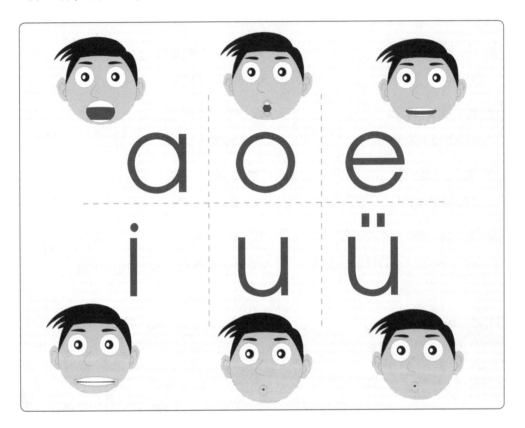

> 2 **Listen to the recording and mark the tones you hear.**
>
> 听一听，标出你听到的声调。

ba	fa	ma	ta
fo	po	bo	mo
ke	de	ge	te
li	bi	yi	ni
fu	pu	mu	bu
nü	yü	lü	

Chinese characters　汉字

1　**Pictures and characters**

图片汉字

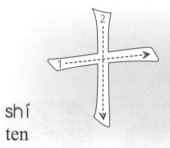

shí
ten

十字　路口
shízì lùkǒu
crossroad

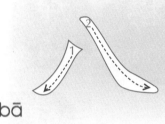

bā
eight

八宝粥
bābǎozhōu
eight treasure congee

2　**Story of Chinese characters**

汉字的故事

How did Chinese characters originate? It is said that over 5 000 years ago, a man named Cang Jie created Chinese characters with his inspiration from the nature in his four eyes. It is only a legend. As a matter of fact, Chinese characters are the work of many people's wisdom.

汉字是怎么产生的呢？传说距今5000年前，有一个人叫仓颉(Cāng Jié)，有四只眼睛，他从看到的世界万物中得到启发创造了文字。这只是一个传说，汉字是很多人的智慧结晶。

仓颉庙
Cāng Jié Miào
Temple of Cang Jie

仓颉
Cāng Jié
Figure of Cang Jie

One Hundred Family Names Primer, a book recording Chinese family names, is a collection of 504 common family names. Actually, there are over 4 000 Chinese family names. According to statistics in 2004, the family name "Li" was the most common one in China.

《百家姓》是中国的一本记录姓氏的书，收集了504个常见的姓。其实，中国的姓大概有4 000多个。2004年，根据统计，姓"李"的人是最多的。

李 Lǐ

刘 Liú

陈 Chén

张 Zhāng

赵 Zhào

周 Zhōu

胡 Hú

吴 Wú

杨 Yáng

徐 Xú

王 Wáng

高 Gāo

孙 Sūn

朱 Zhū

黄 Huáng

What is the family name of your favorite Chinese celebrity? Can you find it from the family names above?

你熟悉的中国明星姓什么？在上面能找到吗？

Chinese community 汉语社区

In various ways, including watching movies, videos, listening to music, or consulting your teachers or your Chinese friends, choose an interesing Chinese name for yourself, and make a Chinese name card. Then show it to everybody in class.

通过各种渠道，包括看电影、录像，听音乐，咨询老师或你的中国朋友，给自己起一个有意思的中国名字，做一张自己的中文名大卡片，并在课堂上展示给大家。

你真好！

Objectives 学习目标

⚫ **Learn to compliment**
学会表达赞美

⚫ **Learn to express your gratitude**
学会表达感谢

Warm-up 热身

Discuss with your partner, and find out which expression may be used to praise these people.
与同伴讨论，看看这些图片可以对应什么样的赞美词？

酷
kù
cool

帅
shuǎi
handsome

漂亮
piàoliang
pretty

可爱
kě'ài
cute

33

Conversation 会 话

你 真 好，谢谢！
Nǐ zhēn hǎo, xièxie!

 1

你 真 漂亮！
Nǐ zhēn piāoliang!

谢谢！
Xièxie!

 2

我 真 帅！
Wǒ zhēn shuài!

 3

 **Words** 词语

真 zhēn	好 hǎo	谢谢 xièxie
very; really	nice, good	thanks
你们 nǐmen	棒 bàng	您 nín
you (plural)	great	you (in polite wa

马丽、李明： 飞飞 真 帅！
Mǎ Lì, Lǐ Míng: Fēifei zhēn shuài!

飞飞： 谢谢 你们！
Fēifei: Xièxie nǐmen!

张 老师： 飞飞，你 真 棒！
Zhāng lǎoshī: Fēifei, nǐ zhēn bàng!

飞飞： 谢谢 您，张 老师！
Fēifei: Xièxie nín, Zhāng lǎoshī!

 Language focus 语言放大镜

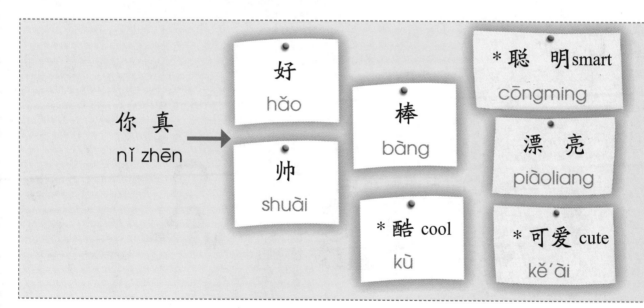

你真 nǐ zhēn →
好 hǎo
帅 shuài
棒 bàng
* 酷 cool kù
* 聪明 smart cōngming
漂亮 piàoliang
* 可爱 cute kě'ài

漂亮 piāoliang pretty	帅 shuài handsome
老师 lǎoshī teacher	

Let's listen 听一听

1 **Listen to the recording, and match the pinyin to the words.**
听录音，为词语选择拼音。

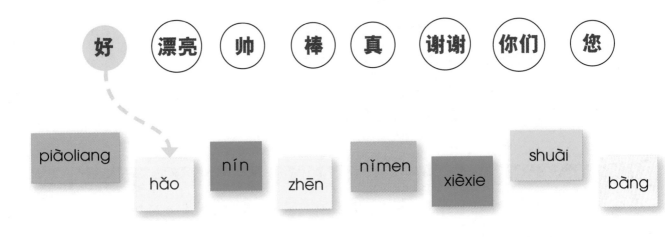

好　漂亮　帅　棒　真　谢谢　你们　您

piāoliang

hǎo　nín　zhēn　nǐmen　xièxie　shuài　bàng

Let's talk 说一说

1 **Follow the example, and talk about the following people with your partner.**
仿照例子，和你的同伴说说下面图片中的人。

① 真可爱!
Zhēn kě'ài!

②

③

④

⑤

⑥

2 **Listen to the recording and choose the sentences you hear.**

听录音，选择你听到的句子。

1 谢谢！
   Xièxie!   再见！
                                           Zàijiàn!

2 你们 真 好！
   Nǐmen zhēn hǎo!   你 真 好！
                                           Nǐ zhēn hǎo!

3 飞飞真 帅！
   Fēifei zhēn shuài!   飞飞真 棒！
                                           Fēifei zhēn bàng!

4 张 红 真 漂亮！
   Zhāng Hóng zhēn piàoliang!   张 红 真 可爱！
                                           Zhāng Hóng zhēn kě'ài!

2 **Talk about your classmates with the words and expressions you've learned.**

用学过的词说一说班里的同学。

Phonetics 语音

1 **Listen and read.**

听一听，读一读。

ai	gāi	bái	mǎi	pài
ei	bēi	péi	měi	lèi
ao	pāo	máo	dǎo	lāo
ou	tōu	lóu	gǒu	hòu

2 **Listen and choose.**

听一听，选一选。

1 mǎi ◯ měi ◯   2 pái ◯ péi ◯

3 gǎi ◯ gěi ◯   4 lài ◯ lèi ◯

5 tāo ◯ tōu ◯   6 máo ◯ móu ◯

7 lǎo ◯ lǒu ◯   8 hào ◯ hòu ◯

3 **Listen to the recording and fill in the blanks.**

听录音，填空。

ai	ei

h___h___   b___b___   m___m___

ao	ou

xiǎot___   xiǎot___   l___l___

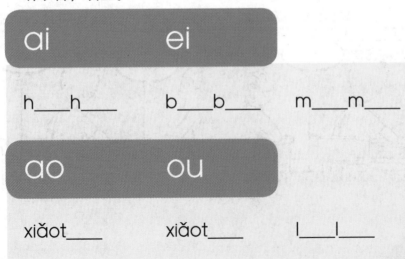

38

Chinese characters 汉　字

1 **Pictures and characters**

图片汉字

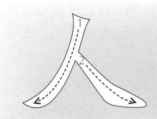

rén
people

人 民 日 报
Rénmín Rìbào
People's Daily

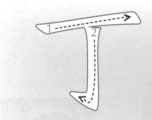

dīng
small cubes; a Chinese surname

宫 保 鸡 丁
Gōngbǎo Jīdīng
fried diced chicken

2 **Story of Chinese characters**

汉字的故事

Do you know what materials the earliest Chinese characters were written on? Over 3 000 years ago, ancient Chinese "wrote" characters on the carapace of tortoises and beast bones. Those characters are called the Oracle-bone-script. The Oracle-bone-script evolved into the current Chinese characters over a period of thousands of years.

你知道最早的汉字写在哪儿吗？3 000多年以前，中国的古人把字写在龟甲和兽骨上，这些文字叫做甲骨文(Jiǎgǔwén)。几千年过去了，甲骨文慢慢演变成了现在的汉字。

甲骨文
Jiǎgǔwén
Oracle-bone-script

China is a country of fifty-six nationalities. Besides Han, there are fifty-five minority groups, such as the Zang, the Hui, and so forth. Many minority groups have kept their own unique traditions, costumes, living habits, etc.

中国是个多民族的国家，一共有56个民族。除了汉族，还有55个少数民族，如藏族、回族等。许多少数民族保留着自己独特的民族传统、文化、服饰和生活习惯等。

壮 族
Zhuàng Zú
Zhuang

维 吾 尔 族
Wéiwú'ěr Zú
Uygur

藏 族
Zàng Zú
Tibetan

苗 族
Miáo Zú
Miao

傣 族
Dǎi Zú
Dai

白 族
Bái Zú
Bai

 Chinese community 汉语社区

Make a small poster with the picture of your family, friend or your favorite celebrity. Write down your praise to him/her in Chinese. Use the poster to introduce him/her to everybody.

做一张小招贴画，向大家介绍你的家人、朋友或你喜欢的明星，选一张他们的照片贴在上面，并用汉语写上你对他们的赞美。

五个香蕉

Objectives 学习目标

- **Learn to enquire and make a request**
  学会询问和提出要求
- **Learn to express quantity in Chinese**
  学会汉语的数量表达法

Warm-up 热身

Look at the following fruits. Which is your favorite? In addition to these, what others do you like?

看看下面的水果，哪个是你最喜欢吃的？除了这些水果，你还喜欢吃什么？

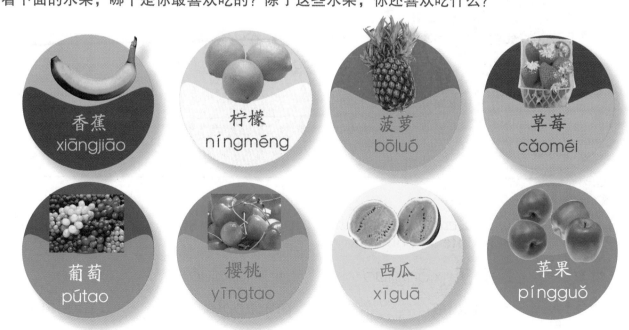

香蕉
xiāngjiāo

柠檬
níngméng

菠萝
bōluó

草莓
cǎoméi

葡萄
pútao

樱桃
yīngtao

西瓜
xīguā

苹果
píngguǒ

Conversation 会话

一、二、三，三个人。
Yī, èr, sān, sān gè rén.

1

我要一个西瓜。
Wǒ yào yí gè xīguā.

2

我要三个 柠檬。
Wǒ yào sān gè níngméng.

3

我要五个香蕉。
Wǒ yào wǔ gè xiāngjiāo.

4

 **Words 词语**

个 gè	人 rén	要 yào
measure word for both people and objects	people, person	want, need
香蕉 xiāngjiāo	菠萝 bōluó	呢 ne
banana	pineapple	a modal particle

老师： 你要 什么？
Lǎoshī： Nǐ yào shénme?

张　红： 我 要一个菠萝，谢谢！
Zhāng Hóng： Wǒ yào yí gè bōluó,　xièxie!

老师： 马丽，你呢？
Lǎoshī： Mǎ Lì,　nǐ ne?

马丽： 我要 两个 苹果，谢谢！
Mǎ Lì： Wǒ yào liǎng gè píngguǒ, xièxie!

 Language focus 语言放大镜

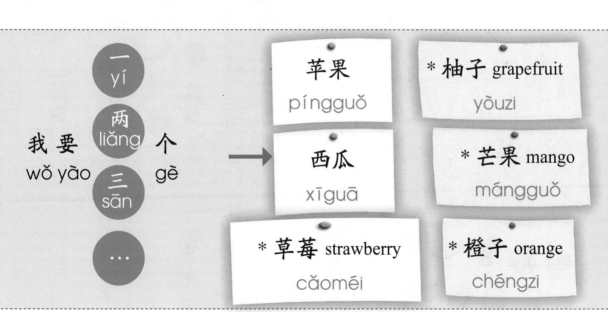

我要 一 yí / 两 liǎng / 三 sān / ... 个 gè → 苹果 píngguǒ / 西瓜 xīguā

*柚子 grapefruit yòuzi
*芒果 mango mángguǒ
*草莓 strawberry cǎoméi
*橙子 orange chéngzi

我要 wǒ yào

西瓜 xīguā watermelon	柠檬 níngméng lemon
两 liǎng two	苹果 píngguǒ apple

Let's listen 听一听

> 1 **Listen to the recording, and match the pictures to the pinyin.**
> 听录音，连接图片和拼音。

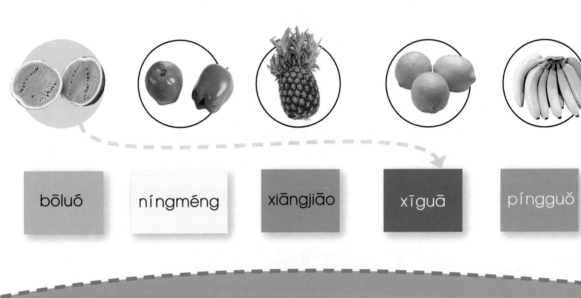

| bōluó | níngméng | xiāngjiāo | xīguā | píngguǒ |

Let's talk 说一说

> 1 **Take a look at the pictures, and then follow the example to complete the dialogue with your partner.**
> 看图片，仿照例句，与同伴完成对话。

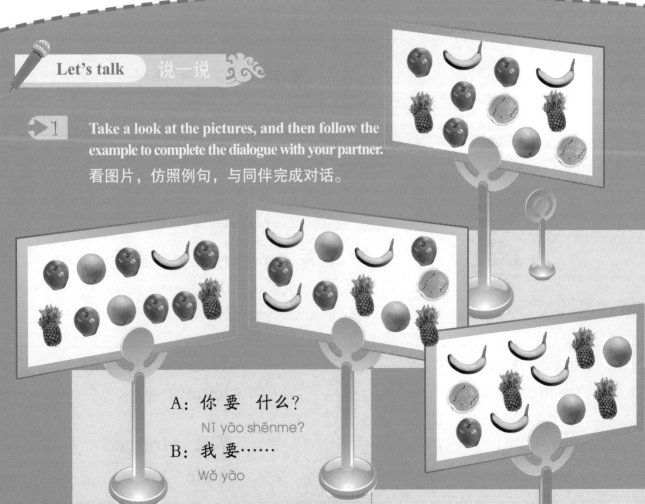

A: 你要 什么？
Nǐ yào shénme?

B: 我要……
Wǒ yào

2 **Listen to the recording and draw the fruits you hear.**

听录音，画出你听到的水果。

2 **Practice after the pictures below. No repetition of the numbers and the fruits is allowed.**

模仿下图的样子做练习，后面的同学不能重复前面的同学说过的数字和水果。

1 **Listen and read.**

听一听，读一读。

an	bān	pán	dǎn	làn
en	fēn	pén	běn	mèn
in	bīn	lín	yǐn	pìn
ang	bāng	máng	fǎng	tàng
eng	bēng	péng	děng	lēng
ing	dīng	píng	bǐng	mìng
ong	dōng	tóng	lǒng	nòng

2 **Listen and write.**

听一听，写一写。

an   ang

f___wèn   f___wèn   xīn f___   xīn f___   l___m___

en   eng

f___dù   f___dù   mù p___   mù p___   f___f___

in   ing

j___jì   j___jì   fù x___   fù x___   x___x___

Chinese characters

1 **Pictures and characters**

图片汉字

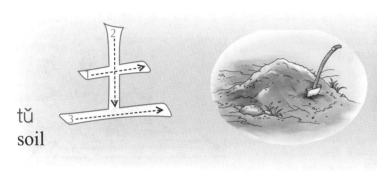

土豆
tǔdòu
potato

tǔ
soil

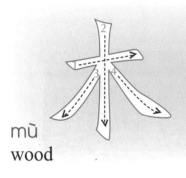

木　地板
mù dìbǎn
wooden floor

mù
wood

2 **Story of Chinese characters**

汉字的故事

Some Chinese characters are like pictures which reflect the shape of things. Match the following characters with the related pictures.

有些汉字就像图画一样，反映了一些东西的形状。试试看，你能不能把下面的汉字和对应的图片连起来。

口　　山　　日　　月

Experiencing China　体验中国

There are a lot of beautiful spots in China. Have a look at the following cities and places. Are you familar with any of them?

中国有很多美丽的地方，看看下面的城市和地方，有没有你熟悉的？

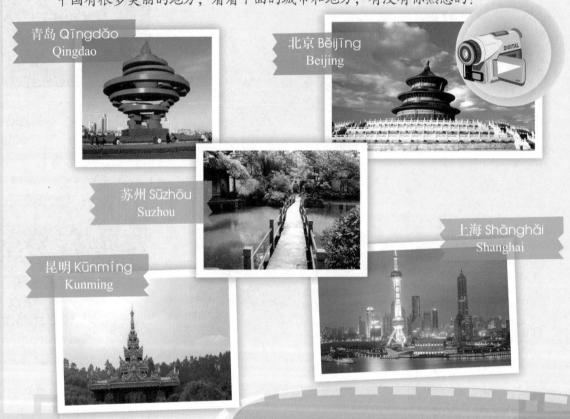

青岛 Qīngdǎo
Qingdao

北京 Běijīng
Beijing

苏州 Sūzhōu
Suzhou

上海 Shànghǎi
Shanghai

昆明 Kūnmíng
Kunming

Are there any places you want to go to in these pictures? What other cities or places do you know?
这些图里有没有你想去的地方？你还知道哪些城市或地方？

Chinese community　汉语社区

我
喜
欢
pútao

Follow the example to make a flash card with your favorite fruit on.

仿照例子，做一张卡片，画出你最喜欢的水果。

我喜欢狗

第 **4** 课

Objectives 学习目标
- **Learn to express what you like**
  学会表达喜爱的感情
- **Learn to express animal names**
  学会表达各种动物的名称

Warm-up 热身

What is your most favorite among the following animals? In addition to these, what others do you like?
你最喜欢下面的什么动物？除了这些动物，还有没有你喜欢的？

老虎 lǎohǔ

熊猫 xiōngmāo

马 mǎ

大象 dàxiàng

狗 gǒu

猫 māo

海豚 hǎitún

考拉 kǎolā

49

Conversation 会话

她喜欢 狗。
Tā xǐhuan gǒu.

我也喜欢 狗。
Wǒ yě xǐhuan gǒu.

1

他喜欢 大象。
Tā xǐhuan dàxiàng.

我也喜欢 大象。
Wǒ yě xǐhuan dàxiàng.

2

它喜欢鱼。
Tā xǐhuan yú.

我也喜欢 鱼。
Wǒ yě xǐhuan yú.

3

Words 词语	他 tā he, him	喜欢 xǐhuan like, be fond of	大象 dàxiàng elephant
	它 tā it	鱼 yú fish	动物 dòngwu animal

李 丁：你喜欢 什么 动物？
Lǐ Dīng： Nǐ xǐhuan shénme dòngwu?

马丽：我喜欢 猫，你呢？
Mǎ Lì： Wǒ xǐhuan māo, nǐ ne?

李 丁：我喜欢 狗。你喜欢 狗 吗？
Lǐ Dīng： Wǒ xǐhuan gǒu.   Nǐ xǐhuan gǒu ma?

马丽：我也喜欢 狗。
Mǎ Lì： Wǒ yě xǐhuan gǒu.

 Language focus 语言放大镜

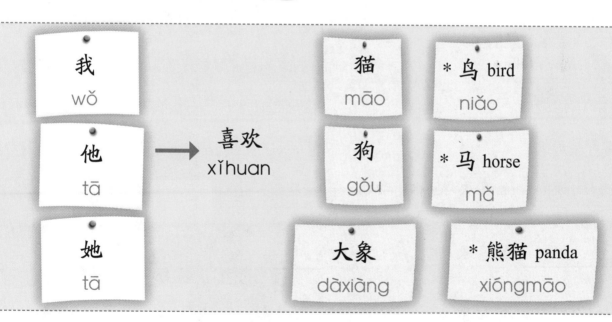

也 yě	她 tā	狗 gǒu
also, either	she, her	dog
猫 māo	吗 ma	
cat	a question particle	

1 Listen to the recording and match the pictures to the words.

听录音，连接图片和词语。

| 鱼 yú | 大象 dàxiāng | 熊猫 xióngmāo | 猫 māo |

Let's talk 说一说

1 Follow the example sentence to ask your classmates what are their favorite animals.

仿照例句，问一问你的同学，他们喜欢什么动物？

A: 你 喜欢 什么 动物？
Nǐ xǐhuan shénme dòngwu?

B: 我 喜欢 狗。
Wǒ xǐhuan gǒu.

A: 我 也 喜欢 狗。
Wǒ yě xǐhuan gǒu.

2 **Listen to the recording and choose the sentences you hear.**

听录音，选择你听到的句子。

1 你喜欢 什么 动物？ □
Nǐ xǐhuan shénme dòngwu?

他喜欢 什么 动物？ □
Tā xǐhuan shénme dòngwu?

2 你喜欢 狗 吗？ □
Nǐ xǐhuan gǒu ma?

你喜欢 猫 吗？ □
Nǐ xǐhuan māo ma?

3 她真 漂亮。 □
Tā zhēn piàoliang.

大象 真 漂亮。 □
Dàxiàng zhēn piàoliang.

4 我喜欢 大象，也喜欢 狗。 □
Wǒ xǐhuan dàxiàng, yě xǐhuan gǒu.

我喜欢 大象，他也喜欢 大象。 □
Wǒ xǐhuan dàxiàng, tā yě xǐhuan dàxiàng.

2 **Form a circle and make sentences. Can you remember what your classmates said?**

围成圈，学说话。你能记住同学的话吗？

他喜欢大象，
我也喜欢大象。

她喜欢狗，
我喜欢大象。

我喜欢狗。

1 **Listen and read.**

听一听，读一读。

ie	piē	bié	miě	liè
ia	qiā	jiá	liǎ	xià
ua	zhuā	huá	kuǎ	guà
uo	tuō	guó	huǒ	luò
üe	quē	jué	lüě	nüè

2 **Listen and read.**

听一听，读一读。

ie   üe
lüèxiě   jiéyuē

ie   ia
xiàjià   jiějiǎ

uo   ua
guóhuā   kuàguó   huāluò   huǒhuā

üan   ian
juànliàn   tiányuán   yuánxiān   xuānyuán

54

Chinese characters   汉字

1 Pictures and characters

图片汉字

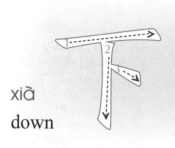

shàng

up

上　车
shàng chē
get on board

xià

down

下 飞机
xià fēijī
get off the airplane

2 Story of Chinese characters

汉字的故事

Chinese characters have been developing for thousands of years. From ancient times to the present they have experienced major evolution from ancient writing, large seal script, small seal script, clerical script, regular script, running script, cursive hand, to Song script. Have a look at these changes.

汉字的发展，经过了几千年的漫长岁月。从古代到今天，汉字一次一次地变化着，历经了古文、大篆、小篆、隶书、楷书、行书、草书、宋体等主要演变过程。看看这些变化吧。

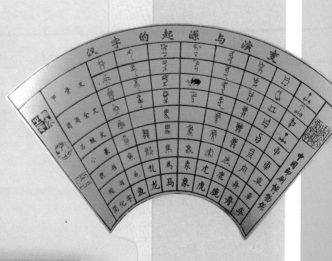

4

Experiencing China 体验中国

There are 12 animals in the Chinese zodiac.
下面是中国的12生肖。

鼠 shǔ
1984, 1996

牛 niú
1985, 1997

虎 hǔ
1986, 1998

兔 tù
1987, 1999

龙 lóng
1988, 2000

蛇 shé
1989, 2001

马 mǎ
1990, 2002

羊 yáng
1991, 2003

猴 hóu
1992, 2004

鸡 jī
1993, 2005

狗 gǒu
1994, 2006

猪 zhū
1995, 2007

In which year were you born? What is the animal of your birth year?
你是哪一年出生的？在中国的生肖里，你属什么？

Chinese community 汉语社区

What pets do your family and neighbors have? What are their names? Relate your observations to your classmates.
你的家人和邻居都养了哪些宠物？他们的宠物叫什么名字，把你的观察结果告诉大家。

复习课1
Review Lesson 1

1 Spell and read.

拼一拼，读一读。

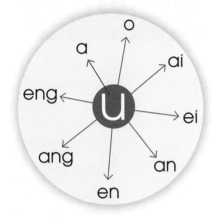

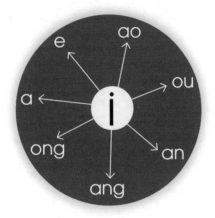

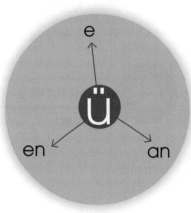

2 Word puzzle.

填字游戏。

			我 wǒ				
			要 yào				
			一 yí				
我 wǒ	要 yào	五 wǔ		香 xiāng	蕉 jiāo		
		西 xī					你 nǐ
李 Lǐ		瓜 guā					要 yào
	你 nǐ	好 hǎo					什 shén
她 tā		漂 piào	亮 liang		她 tā	叫 jiào	什 shén	
	好 hǎo			我 wǒ		飞 fēi	飞 fei
			王 Wáng	老 lǎo	师 shī		见 jiàn

3 Use the following words to make as many sentences as possiable.

用下面的词组句子，看谁组的句子多。

我 wǒ	西瓜 xīguā	柠檬 níngmé
张老师 Zhāng lǎoshī	苹果 píngguǒ	香蕉 xiāngjiāc
他 tā 喜欢 xǐhuan	菠萝 bōluó	大象 dàxiàng
她 tā	狗 gǒu	鱼 yú
它 tā	猫 māo	

4 Sing a song.

唱一唱。

飞飞喜欢 吃香蕉，

柠檬西瓜 和菠萝。

多吃水果身 体 好，

聪明可爱 个子高。

飞飞聪明个 子 高，

多 吃 水 果 身 体 好。

58

我的眼睛很大

Objectives 学习目标

○ **Learn to describe one's appearance**
学会描述一个人的相貌

Match the words with the picture in the middle, and talk about the part of your body you are most satisfied with.

连接词语和身体的部位，说说你最满意自己的什么部位。

 鼻子 bízi

 头发 tóufa

眼睛 yǎnjing

 嘴 zuǐ

 耳朵 ěrduo

我 的 眼睛 很 大。
Wǒ de yǎnjing hěn dà.

我 的 眼睛 也 很 大。
Wǒ de yǎnjing yě hěn dà.

1

我 的 个子 很 高。
Wǒ de gèzi hěn gāo.

我 的 个子 也 很 高。
Wǒ de gèzi yě hěn gāo.

2

我 的 头发 很 长。
Wǒ de tóufa hěn cháng.

我 的 头发 也 很 长。
Wǒ de tóufa yě hěn cháng.

3

Words 词语

的 de possessive particle	眼睛 yǎnjing eye	很 hěn very
头发 tóufa hair	长 cháng long	名字 míngzi name

张　红：李明，你的狗叫什么名字？
Zhāng Hóng: Lǐ Míng, nǐ de gǒu jiào shénme míngzi?

李　明：它叫笨笨。
Lǐ Míng: Tā jiào Bēnben.

张　红：笨笨的眼睛大吗？
Zhāng Hóng: Bēnben de yǎnjing dà ma?

李　明：它的眼睛很大，嘴也很大。
Lǐ Míng: Tā de yǎnjing hěn dà, zuǐ yě hěn dà.

张　红：眼睛很大，嘴也很大。真可爱。
Zhāng Hóng: Yǎnjing hěn dà, zuǐ yě hěn dà. Zhēn kě'ài.

 Language focus　语言放大镜

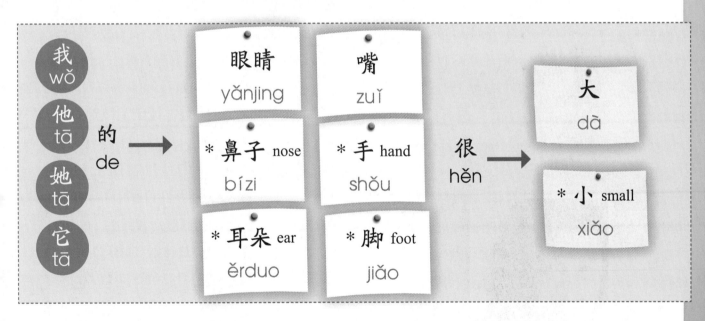

大 dà	个子 gèzi	高 gāo
big	stature	high
嘴 zuǐ		
mouth		

Let's listen 听一听

> 1 **Listen to the recording and match the pictures to the words.**
> 听录音，连线。

| 大
dà | 高
gāo | 漂亮
piàoliang | 长
cháng | 可爱
kě'ài |

Let's talk 说一说

> 1 **Choose pictures of your favorite people and paste them in the spaces below. Then describe them to your partner by imitating the example sentences.**
> 挑选你喜欢的人物的照片，把它们贴在下面，仿照例句，向你的同伴进行描述。

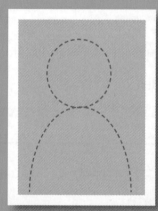

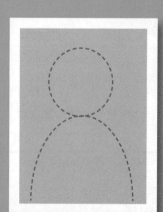

我喜欢王力宏的眼睛。
他的眼睛很漂亮。

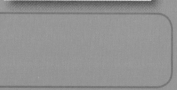

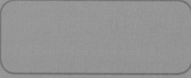

2 **Listen to the recording and choose the sentences you hear.**

听录音，选择你听到的句子。

① 大象 的鼻子很 大。
Dàxiàng de bízi hěn dà.

大象 的鼻子很 长。
Dàxiàng de bízi hěn cháng.

② 她的个子高 吗？
Tā de gèzi gāo ma?

她的个子很 高。
Tā de gèzi hěn gāo.

③ 李明 的 眼睛 真 漂亮。
Lǐ Míng de yǎnjing zhēn piàoliang.

李明 的嘴真 漂亮。
Lǐ Míng de zuǐ zhēn piàoliang.

④ 我 喜欢 她的头发。
Wǒ xǐhuan tā de tóufa.

我 喜欢 我 的头发。
Wǒ xǐhuan wǒ de tóufa.

2 **Cut out the picture on the insert, and play the "jigsaw puzzle game" with your classmates.**

剪下插页上的图片，跟同学们一起做"拼图游戏"。

1 **Listen and read.**

听一听，读一读。

j	jiā	jí	jiǎn	jù
q	qū	qiú	qiǎn	qiàng
x	xiū	xiáng	xiǎn	xià

2 **Pronounce the following words.**

开口试一试。

xuéxí　jìjiāqì　xǐjí'érqì

jìxìn　qīxījié　xīngxīngxiāngxī

3 **Tongue twister.**

绕口令。

Yí gè xiǎo háizi,

ná shuāng xīn xiézi;

kàn jiàn dà qiézi,

fàng xia xīn xiézi;

qù shí dà qiézi,

diū le xīn xiézi.

Chinese characters   汉　字

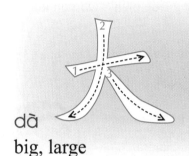 **1**   **Pictures and characters**

图片汉字

dà
big, large

北京　大学
Běijīng Dàxué
Peking University

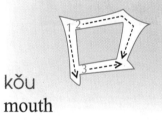

kǒu
mouth

出口
chūkǒu
exit

2   **Story of Chinese characters**

汉字的故事

Chinese characters consist of many radicals, among which some are meaningful. Characters with the same radical may have related meanings. For example, characters with 木 as the radical are related to wood; characters with 水 as the radical are related to water. Think about the meanings of the radicals below.

汉字由许多偏旁组成，有的偏旁能代表意义。有相同偏旁的字，意思有可能相关。例如：“木”做偏旁的字，与树木有关系；“水（氵）”做偏旁的字多和水有关系。想一想，下面这些偏旁会表示什么意义呢？

The Great Wall is a landmark of China. The earliest "Great Wall", built in the Qin Dynasty, experienced extensions and repairs many times afterward. As the saying is, "He who does not reach the Great Wall is not a true man". Do you know who first said it?

长城是中国的一个标志性建筑。最早的"万里长城"是秦朝时连接起来的，后来又经历了许多次修建。有句话叫"不到长城非好汉"，你知道是谁说的吗？

秦长城遗址
Qín Chángchéng yízhǐ
The remains of the great walls of the Qin state of the Warring States period

八达岭长城
Bādálǐng Chángchéng
Badaling Great Wall

嘉峪关
Jiāyù Guān
Jiayu Pass

Have you, your family, or friends been to the Great Wall? Do you know other stories about the Great Wall?
你或你的家人、朋友有没有去过长城？你知道有关长城的其他故事吗？

Chinese community 汉语社区

Perfect image—collect photos of your favorite celebrities, use sentences you have learned to describe their most charming facial features, and then gather the charming facial features from different celebrities to create a "perfect image".

完美形象——搜集一些自己喜欢的明星的照片，用学过的语句介绍他们最有魅力的五官部位，然后，把你喜欢的来自不同明星的魅力五官凑在一起，制造一个"完美形象"。

这是我妈妈

Objectives 学习目标
- **Learn to express relatives' titles**
  学会表达亲属称谓

Warm-up 热身

Talk about the relationships among the people in the picture.
说说图中人物的关系。

爷爷 yéye
grandfather

奶奶 nǎinai
grandmother

爸爸 bàba
father

妈妈 māma
mother

姐姐 jiějie
older sister

弟弟 dìdi
younger brother

Mǎ Ruì是Mǎ Wěi的_____。

Mǎ Ruì是Mǎ Huá的_____。

Mǎ Tíng是Mǎ Wěi的_____。

Wáng Lì是Mǎ Tíng的_____。

67

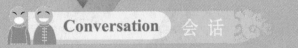

这 是 我 妈妈，她 很 漂亮。
Zhè shì wǒ māma, tā hěn piàoliang.

这 是 我 爸爸，他 很 帅。
Zhè shì wǒ bàba, tā hěn shuài.

1

这 是 我 哥哥。他 很 高。
Zhè shì wǒ gēge. Tā hěn gāo.

那 是 我 姐姐。她 的 头发 很 长。
Nà shì wǒ jiějie. Tā de tóufa hěn cháng.

2

这 是 我 弟弟。
Zhè shì wǒ dìdi.

那 是 我 妹妹。
Nà shì wǒ mèimei.

3

	这 zhè this	妈妈 māma mother	爸爸 bàba father
Words **词语**	姐姐 jiějie older sister	弟弟 dìdi younger brother	妹妹 mèimei younger sister

李 丁： 这 是 谁?
Lǐ Dīng:　Zhè shì shuí?

马 丽： 这 是 我 哥哥。
Mǎ Lì:　Zhè shì wǒ gēge.

李 丁： 他 真 帅! 他是 学生 吗?
Lǐ Dīng:　Tā zhēn shuài!　Tā shì xuésheng ma?

马 丽： 他是 学生。
Mǎ Lì:　Tā shì xuésheng.

李 丁： 那是 谁?
Lǐ Dīng:　Nà shì shuí?

马 丽： 那是 我 哥哥的 朋友。他也是 学生。
Mǎ Lì:　Nà shì wǒ gēge de péngyou. Tā yě shì xuésheng.

 Language focus 语言放大镜

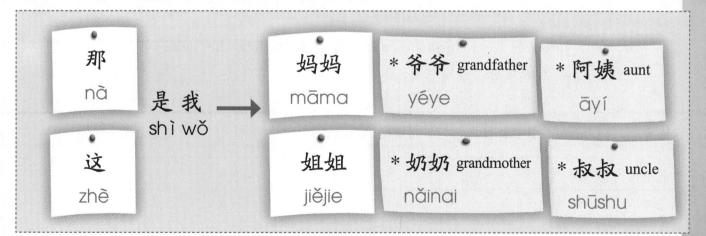

那
nà

这
zhè

 是我
shì wǒ →

妈妈
māma

*爷爷 grandfather
yéye

*阿姨 aunt
āyí

姐姐
jiějie

*奶奶 grandmother
nǎinai

*叔叔 uncle
shūshu

哥哥 gēge		那 nà
older brother		that
谁 shuí	学生 xuésheng	朋友 péngyou
who	student	friend

Let's listen 听一听

> 1 **Listen and link.**
>
> 听录音，连线。

Let's talk 说一说

> 1 **Interview three classmates, and then fill in the following table.**
>
> 采访3位同学，填写下表：

Classmates' names	Family members	Characteristics

2 **Listen to the recording and choose the sentences you hear.**

听录音，选择你听到的句子。

① 这 是 谁？　　　　这 是 什么？
Zhè shì shuí?　　　　Zhè shì shénme?

② 这 是 他的 朋友。　　这 是 爸爸的 朋友。
Zhè shì tā de péngyou.　　Zhè shì bàba de péngyou.

③ 我 喜欢 姐姐。　　姐姐喜欢 我。
Wǒ xǐhuan jiějie.　　Jiějie xǐhuan wǒ.

④ 李 明 是我哥哥。　　李 明 是我弟弟。
Lǐ Míng shì wǒ gēge.　　Lǐ Míng shì wǒ dìdi.

⑤ 爸爸的鼻子很 高。　　爸爸的鼻子很 大。
Bàba de bízi hěn gāo.　　Bàba de bízi hěn dà.

2 **Introduce your family to the class.**

跟全班同学介绍一下你的家人。

这 是 我 爸爸。
Zhè shì wǒ bàba.
这 是 我 妈妈。
Zhè shì wǒ māma.
这 是 我。
Zhè shì wǒ.

Phonetics 语 音

 Listen and read.

听一听，读一读。

zh	zhū	zhé	zhǐ	zhǎn
ch	chī	cháng	chǔ	chà
sh	shāng	shí	shǔ	shài
r		rú	rě	rōu

2 **Pronounce the following words.**

开口试一试。

chūzūchē chéngshí

rìzhàoshì zhūchù

3 **Listen and write.**

听一听，写一写。

___ā jiǎo
___ā jiǎo

___á ___í
___ā ___í

___áo ___ù
___ǎo ___ù

___ū ___ù
___ù ___ù

Chinese characters 汉 字

1 **Pictures and characters**

图片汉字

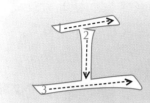

gōng
worker, work

工商   银行
Gōngshāng Yínháng
Industrial and
Commercial Bank

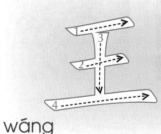

wáng
king; a Chinese surname

王致和   （豆腐乳）
Wángzhìhé(dòufurǔ)

2 **Story of Chinese characters**

汉字的故事

　　Mainland Chinese used traditional Chinese characters in the past, but now China has simplified characters which are easy to remember and write. In Hong Kong, Macao, and Taiwan, the traditional Chinese characters are still used; therefore, there is a coexistence of traditional and simplified Chinese characters. Have a look at these traditional and simplified Chinese characters.

　　原来中国使用的是繁体字，现在国家制定出了易记、易写、简单的汉字——简体字，在港、澳、台地区还一直保留使用繁体字，于是出现了繁体字和简体字并存使用的现状。看一看这些字的简体和繁体吧。

漢語——汉语　**中國**——中国　**學習**——学习

Confucius was a great Chinese ideologist, politician, and educator. He paid much attention to the proprieties of daily life. He left a lot of instructive idioms, such as "when you are together with two other people, at least one can be your teacher in some way."

孔子(Kǒngzǐ)是中国伟大的思想家、政治家和教育家。他非常注重日常生活中的礼节，留下了许多有益的思想，比如"三人行必有我师"。

孔林 Kǒnglín
The Cemetery of Confucius

孔府 Kǒngfǔ
The Confucian Mansion

孔子像
Kǒngzǐ xiàng
A Portrait of Confucius

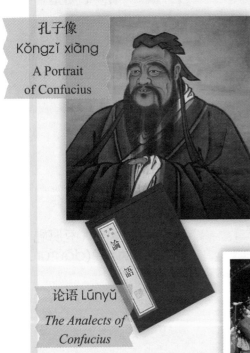

孔庙 Kǒngmiào
The Temple of Confucius

论语 Lúnyǔ
The Analects of Confucius

孔子艺术节
Kǒngzǐ yìshu Jié
The Confucius Art Festival

What else do you know about Confucius?
关于孔子，你还知道什么？

Chinese community 汉语社区

Draw your family tree using Chinese to clearly indicate the relationships between you and each of your relatives.

画一张自己家庭成员的树形图，用汉语写清楚每一位亲属与自己的关系。

看，我的电脑

Objectives 学习目标

○ **Learn to describe the position of objects**
学会描述物体的位置

Warm-up 热身

Identify the differences between the two pictures.

找一找，下面的两张画有几处不同？

1

2

 **Conversation** 会 话

看，这是我的电脑，电脑
Kàn, zhè shì wǒ de diànnǎo, diànnǎo

在桌子的 上边。
zài zhuōzi de shàngbian.

 1

看，那是哥哥的足球，足球
Kàn, nà shì gēge de zúqiú, zúqiú

在桌子的 下边。
zài zhuōzi de xiàbian.

 2

看，那是姐姐的书，书也在
Kàn, nà shì jiějie de shū, shū yě zài

桌子的 下边。
zhuōzi de xiàbian.

 3

Words 词语	看 kàn look	电脑 diànnǎo computer	在 zài be in/at/on
	下边 xiàbian below	书 shū book	哪儿 nǎr where

李 明： 妈妈，我的书在哪儿？
Lǐ Míng: Māma, wǒ de shū zài nǎr?

妈妈： 书在桌子的 上边，电脑 旁边。
Māma: Shū zài zhuōzi de shàngbian, diànnǎo pángbiān.

李明： 我的手机在哪儿？
Lǐ Míng: Wǒ de shǒujī zài nǎr?

妈妈： 手机在书的 旁边。
Māma: Shǒujī zài shū de pángbiān.

 Language focus 语言放大镜

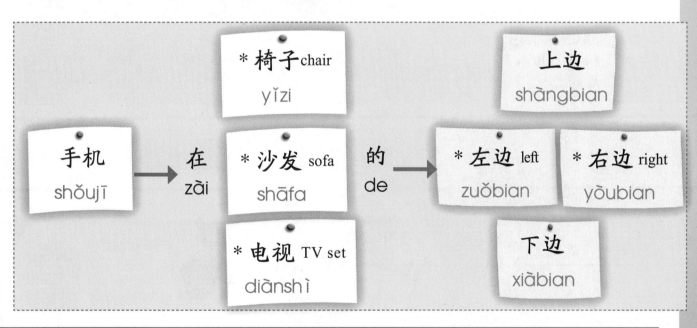

桌子 zhuōzi	上边 shàngbian	足球 zúqiú
table	above	football
手机 shǒujī	旁边 pángbiān	
cell phone	side	

Let's listen 听一听

> 1 **Listen to the recording and draw the position of the objects.**
>
> 听录音，画出物品的位置。

Let's talk 说一说

> 1 **Follow the example sentence and talk about the things in the picture.**
>
> 仿照例句，看图说话。

这 是 鱼。鱼 在 桌子 的
Zhè shì yú. Yú zài zhuōzi de
上边。
shàngbian.

Listen to the recording and choose the sentences you hear.

听录音，选择你听到的句子。

① 看，这是我的手机。
Kàn, zhè shì wǒ de shǒujī.

看，这是我的 电脑。
Kàn, zhè shì wǒ de diànnǎo.

② 我的猫在桌子 上边。
Wǒ de māo zài zhuōzi shàngbian.

我的猫在桌子下边。
Wǒ de māo zài zhuōzi xiàbian.

③ 我的足球在哪儿？
Wǒ de zúqiú zài nǎr?

足球在桌子下边 吗？
Zúqiú zài zhuōzi xiàbian ma?

④ 姐姐的手机在 电脑 上边。
Jiějie de shǒujī zài diànnǎo shàngbian.

姐姐的手机在 电脑 旁边。
Jiějie de shǒujī zài diànnǎo pángbiān.

 Cut out the picture on the insert, and play the "jigsaw puzzle game" with your classmates.

剪下插页上的图片，与同学们一起做"拼图游戏"。

Phonetics 语音

1 **Listen and read.**

听一听，读一读。

Z	zāi	zé	zǎo	zuò
C	cā	cáo	cǎn	cuò
S	sāng	sú	sǎ	sān

2 **Pronounce the following words.**

开口试一试。

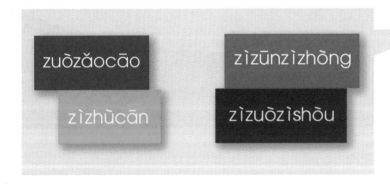

zuòzǎocāo

zìzūnzìzhòng

zìzhùcān

zìzuòzìshòu

3 **Listen and write.**

听一听，写一写。

＿＿á ＿＿ǎo
＿＿ā ＿＿ǎo

＿＿ǎo mù
＿＿ǎo mù

＿＿ì ＿＿ī
＿＿ī ＿＿ì

＿＿ì ＿＿ì
＿＿ì ＿＿í

Chinese characters　汉字

1　Pictures and characters

图片汉字

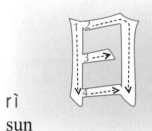

rì
sun

生日
shēngrì
birthday

yuè
moon

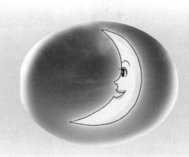

月饼
yuèbǐng
mooncake

2　Story of Chinese characters

汉字的故事

There are many methods to input Chinese characters on a computer, some of which are based on Pinyin, while others are based on strokes. The common Chinese characters input methods include: Microsoft Pinyin Input method, UNIS Pinyin Input method, Intelligent ABC Input method and WBX Input method.

电脑输入汉字有很多方法，有的根据拼音来输入，有的根据笔画。现在比较常见的汉字输入法有：微软拼音输入法、清华紫光拼音输入法、智能ABC输入法、五笔字型输入法等等。

Experiencing China 体验中国

长江是中国的第一长河，全长6 300多公里；黄河是第二长河，全长
5 300多公里。在中国，这两条河被称为"母亲河"。

The Yangtze River, over 6 300 kms, is the longest river in China; the Yellow
River, over 5 300 kms, is the second longest river in China, In China, the two
rivers are called "the Mother Rivers".

长江
Chángjiāng
Yangtze River

黄河小浪底
Huánghé Xiǎolàngdǐ
Yellow River Xiaolangdi

三峡工程
Sānxiá Gōngchéng
The Three Gorges Project

黄河
Huánghé
Yellow River

Do you know why the two rivers are called the "the Mother
Rivers"?
你知道为什么这两条河叫"母亲河"吗？

Chinese community 汉语社区

Each student draws a picture or takes a photo
of his/her desk at home, makes a poster, and then
communicates with other students.

每个同学画一张，或者用数码相机拍一张自己家里书
桌的照片，制作一张招贴画，与其他同学交流一下。

这不是你的书包

Objectives 学习目标

⭕ **Learn to apologize and respond to apologies**
学会表达道歉与回应

⭕ **Learn to express negation**
学会表达否定

Warm-up 热身

What is in your bag? Please place a tick beside the articles you have in your bag, and describe the other articles in your bag.

你的书包里有哪些物品？请在相应的物品旁边打钩，并说说书包里还有什么其他物品。

尺子
chǐzi

橡皮
xiàngpí

MP3

笔
bǐ

笔袋
bǐdài

手机
shǒujī

笔记本
bǐjìběn

书
shū

那不是你的书包，是我的书包。
Nà bú shì nǐ de shūbāo, shì wǒ de shūbāo.

对不起。
Duìbuqǐ.

没关系。
Méi guānxi.

 1

那不是你们班的本子，是我们
Nà bú shì nǐmen bān de běnzi,   shì wǒmen

班的本子。
bān de běnzi.

对不起。
Duìbuqǐ.

没关系。
Méi guānxi.

2

这是谁的笔? 是你的笔吗?
Zhè shì shuí de bǐ?   Shì nǐ de bǐ ma?

这不是我的笔，是老师的笔。
Zhè bú shì wǒ de bǐ,   shì lǎoshī de bǐ.

3

**Words
词语**

不 bù	书包 shūbāo	对不起 duìbuqǐ
no, not	schoolbag	sorry
本子 běnzi	笔 bǐ	课本 kèběn
notebook	pen	textbook

张　红： 这是你的课本吗?
Zhāng Hóng: Zhè shì nǐ de kèběn ma?

王飞飞： 这不是我的课本，我的课本在书包里。
Wáng Fēifei: Zhè bú shì wǒ de kèběn, wǒ de kèběn zài shūbāo lǐ.

张　红： 这是谁的课本?
Zhāng Hóng: Zhè shì shuí de kèběn?

王飞飞： 我不知道。
Wáng Fēifei: Wǒ bù zhīdào.

Language focus 语言放大镜

这不是我的
zhè bú shì wǒ de　→

* 钢笔 fountain pen
gāngbǐ

* 橡皮 eraser
xiàngpí

本子
běnzi

* 铅笔 pencil
qiānbǐ

* 圆珠笔 ball-point pen
yuánzhūbǐ

* 尺子 ruler
chǐzi

没关系 méi guānxi	班 bān
don't worry about it; no problem	class
里 lǐ	知道 zhīdào
in, inside	know

1 Listen to the recording and mark the order in which you hear the words and expressions.

听录音，写出你听到的顺序。

1 我们 ☐ 你们 ☐ 他们 ☐
wǒmen   nǐmen   tāmen

2 对不起 ☐ 没 关系 ☐ 谢谢 ☐
duìbuqǐ   méi guānxi   xièxie

3 笔 ☐ 本子 ☐ 书包 ☐
bǐ   běnzi   shūbāo

4 老师 的笔 ☐ 你的 书包 ☐ 你的本子 ☐
lǎoshī de bǐ   nǐ de shūbāo   nǐ de běnzi

Let's talk 说一说

1 Change the following sentences into negative ones.

把下面的句子变成否定句。

1. 我叫飞飞。 Wǒ jiào Fēifei.   2. 这是马丽的姐姐。 Zhè shì Mǎ Lì de jiějie.

3. 李明很帅。 Lǐ Míng hěn shuài.   4. 这是老师的笔。 Zhè shì lǎoshī de bǐ.

5. 我的眼睛很大。 Wǒ de yǎnjing hěn dà. 6. 他的课本在书包里。 Tā de kèběn zài shūbāo lǐ.

7. 我的个子很高。 Wǒ de gèzi hěn gāo. 8. 我喜欢看电视。 Wǒ xǐhuan kàn diànshì.

9. 他喜欢大象，我也喜欢大象。 Tā xǐhuan dàxiàng, wǒ yě xǐhuan dàxiàng.

> 2 **Listen to the recording and fill in the blanks.**
> 听录音，填空。

① 那＿＿＿＿＿你的＿＿＿＿＿。
　Nà　　　　　nǐ de

② ＿＿＿＿＿。
　没关系。
　Méiguānxi.

③ 那是＿＿＿＿＿的笔。
　Nà shì　　　　de bǐ.

④ 那是＿＿＿＿＿的本子。
　Nà shì　　　　de běnzi.

> 3 **Listen to the recording and decide whether the following statements are true or false.**
> 听录音，判断对错。

① 他 不 帅。
　Tā bú shuài.　　　　　　　□

② 他 不 喜欢　大象，喜欢　狗。
　Tā bù xǐhuan dàxiàng, xǐhuan gǒu.　□

③ 哥哥 的 个子不 高，眼睛 不大。
　Gēge de gèzi bù gāo, yǎnjing bú dà.　□

④ 姐姐的 书 在 桌子 下边。
　Jiějie de shū zài zhuōzi xiàbian.　□

> 2 **Collect everyone's stationery, and then ask the students which is theirs.**
> 把大家的文具收上来，问一问，看一看，哪一个文具是你自己的?

1 **Listen, write, and read.**

听一听，写一写，读一读。

z	zh

___āo ___ǐ ___uǒ___ǔ

c	ch

___ā ___uāng ___ū___ūn

s	sh

___àng ___ù ___uǎn___ù

2 **Tongue twister.**

绕口令。

四是四，十是十，
Sì shì sì, shí shì shí,

十四是十四；
shísì shì shísì,

四十是四十。
sìshí shì sìshí.

十四不是四十；
shísì bú shì sìshí;

四十不是十四。
sìshí bú shì shísì.

Chinese characters　汉字

1
Pictures and characters

图片汉字

shān
mountain

泰山
Tāishān
Taishan Mount

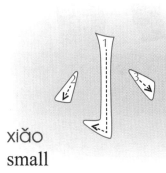

小提琴
xiǎotíqín
violin

xiǎo
small

2
Story of Chinese characters

汉字的故事

Chinese character is not just tool for written communication among Chinese, but also a kind of unique art. Chinese calligraphy has been gradually created during centuries of practical writing and has become an important part of Chinese culture. Appreciate the following works.

汉字不仅是中国人书写交流的工具，它本身还是一种独特的造型艺术。人们书写应用汉字的过程中，逐渐产生了中国书法，成为中国文化的一部分。欣赏一下下面的作品吧。

龙
lóng

天道　酬勤
tiāndào chóuqín

中国功夫包括中国武术和气功，是体育运动，又是一种艺术。

Chinese kungfu, which includes Chinese Wushu and Qigong, is both a sport and an art.

少林　功夫
shàolín gōngfu
Shaolin Kungfu

功夫　明星　——李　小龙
gōngfu míngxīng——Lǐ Xiǎolóng
Kungfu star — Li Xiaolong

太极　拳
tàijí quán
Taiji

Are there any Chinese Kungfu stars you are familiar with?
有没有你熟悉的中国功夫明星？

 Chinese community 汉语社区

Count the number of your personal objects (such as cell phone, textbook, and pen), and then make a statistical table by using a computer.

统计一下自己个人物品（比如手机、课本、笔等物品）的数量，用电脑做一个统计表。

复习课2
Review Lesson 2

1 Listen, write, and read.

听一听，写一写，读一读。

r l	__āng__ù	__ái__én	__ì__ì	__à__òu
x sh	__ī__ī	__í__í	__iān__í	__í__iān
k h	__ē yào	__ē xué	__àn__ǎo	__àn__ǎo
j q x	__í__ī　__ì__ī	__ī__í　__ī__ì	__í__í	__í__ì

2 Word puzzle.

填字游戏。

			那 nà				
	这 zhè		我 wǒ	姐 jiě	姐 jiě		
你 nǐ		谁 shuí			姐 jie		
	谁 shuí		眼 yǎn	睛 jing		大 dà	猫 māo
				喜 xǐ			
	哥 gē	书 shū		欢 huan	我 wǒ		椅 yǐ
	哥 ge	包 bāo		我 wǒ			子 zi
	的 de		对 duì		本 běn		下 xià
		机 jī		在 zài	桌 zhuō	上 shàng	
	很 hěn		起 qi		在 zài		
	大 dà				哪 nà		
			你 nǐ	在 zài	哪 nǎ		

91

3 Use the following words to form sentences as quickly as possiable.

用下面的词连句子，看谁做的快。

哪儿 nǎr　在 zài　你 nǐ

你们 nǐmen　谁 shuí　是 shì

谁 shuí　的 de　电脑 diànnǎo　是 shì　这 zhè

眼睛 yǎnjing　不 bù　的 de　姐姐 jiějie　大 dà

上边 shàngbian　不 bù　手机 shǒujī　在 zài　的 de　桌子 zhuōzi

4 Make up a story as interesting as possible with the following words，and type it out on the computer.

用下面的字编一个故事，用电脑打出来，看看谁编的故事最有意思。

大	口	王	山	小	月

参 考 译 文
Translation Reference

1 你 好   Hello!

你好！我是飞飞。   Hello, I am Feifei.
你好，fēifei!   Hello, Feifei!

你好！我是飞飞。   Hello, I am Feifei.
Fēifei，你好！   Feifei, hello!

你好！我是飞飞。   Hello, I am Feifei.
飞飞，你好。   Feifei, hello.

再见，fēifei!   Goodbye, Feifei!
再见！   Goodbye!

王飞飞：你好，我叫飞飞，你叫什么？   Wang Feifei: Hello. I am Feifei. What's your name?
李 明：我姓李，叫李明。飞飞，你姓什么？   Li Ming: My last name is Li, and my full name is Li Ming. Feifei, may I have your family name?
王飞飞：我姓王。   Wang Feifei: My family name is Wang.

2 你 真 好   It's very nice of you!

你真好，谢谢！   It's very nice of you, thanks!

你真漂亮！   You are very beautiful!

谢谢！   Thank you!

我真帅！　　　　　　　　　　I'm handsome!

马丽、李明：飞飞真帅！　　　　Ma Li, Li Ming:　Feifei, you are very handsome!
　　飞　飞：谢谢你们！　　　　　　　　Feifei:　Thank you!
　　张老师：飞飞，你真棒！　　Madame Zhang:　Feifei, well done!
　　飞　飞：谢谢您，张老师！　　　　　Feifei:　Thank you! Madame Zhang!

3 五 个 香 蕉　　　Five bananas

一、二、三，三个人。　　　　One, two, three, three persons.

我要一个西瓜。　　　　　　　I want a watermelon.

我要三个柠檬。　　　　　　　I want three lemons.

我要五个香蕉。　　　　　　　I want five bananas.

老　师：你要什么？　　　　　Teacher:　What do you want?
张　红：我要一个菠萝，谢谢！　Zhang Hong:　I want a pineapple, thanks!
老　师：马丽，你呢？　　　　Teacher:　Ma Li, what about you?
马　丽：我要两个苹果，谢谢！　　Ma Li:　I want two apples. Thank you!

4 我喜欢狗　　　I like dogs

她喜欢狗。　　　　　　　　　She likes dogs.
我也喜欢狗。　　　　　　　　I like dogs too.

他喜欢大象。　　　　　　　　He likes elephants.

我也喜欢大象。	I like elephants too.
它喜欢鱼。	It likes fish.
我也喜欢鱼。	I like fish too.

李丁：你喜欢什么动物？	Li Ding: What is your favorite animal?
马丽：我喜欢猫，你呢？	Ma Li: I like cats. What about you?
李丁：我喜欢狗。你喜欢狗吗？	Li Ding: I like dogs. Do you like dogs?
马丽：我也喜欢狗。	Ma Li: Yes, I do.

5 我的眼睛很大　　　　I have big eyes

我的眼睛很大。	I have big eyes.
我的眼睛也很大。	I have big eyes, too.
我的个子很高。	I am very tall.
我的个子也很高。	I am very tall, too.
我的头发很长。	I have long hair.
我的头发也很长。	I have long hair, too.

张红：李明，你的狗叫什么名字？	Zhang Hong: Li Ming, what is your dog's name?
李明：它叫笨笨。	Li Ming: It is called Benben.
张红：笨笨的眼睛大吗？	Zhang Hong: Does it have wide eyes?
李明：它的眼睛很大，嘴也很大。	Li Ming: Yeah. It has wide eyes and a large mouth.
张红：眼睛很大，嘴也很大。真可爱。	Zhang Hong: Wide eyes and large mouth. It is so cute.

6 这是我妈妈

This is my mother

这是我妈妈，她很漂亮。
这是我爸爸，他很帅。

This is my mother, and she's very beautiful.
This is my father, and he's very handsome.

这是我哥哥。他很高。
那是我姐姐。她的头发很长。

This is my older brother. He's tall.
That is my older sister. She has long hair.

这是我弟弟。
那是我妹妹。

This is my little brother.
That is my little sister.

李丁：这是谁?
马丽：这是我哥哥。
李丁：他真帅！他是学生吗?
马丽：他是学生。
李丁：那是谁?
马丽：那是我哥哥的朋友。他也是
　　　学生。

Li Ding:　Who is this?
　Ma Li:　This is my older brother.
Li Ding:　He is so handsome. Is he a student?
　Ma Li:　Yeah!
Li Ding:　Who is that?
　Ma Li:　That is my brother's friend. He is
　　　　　also a student.

7 看，我的电脑

Look, my computer

看，这是我的电脑，电脑在桌子的
上边。

Look, this is my computer. It's on the desk.

看，那是哥哥的足球，足球在桌子的
下边。

Look, that is my older brother's football. It's under the desk.

看，那是姐姐的书，书也在桌子的
下边。

Look, that is my older sister's book. It's also under the desk.

李明：妈妈，我的书在哪儿？
妈妈：书在桌子的上边，电脑旁边。
李明：我的手机在哪儿？
妈妈：手机在书的旁边。

Li Ming: Mom, where is my book?
    Mum: It's on the desk, beside the computer.
Li Ming: Where is my cell phone?
    Mum: It's beside the book.

8 这不是你的书包

This is not your bag

那不是你的书包，是我的书包。
对不起。
没关系。

That is not your bag, it's mine.
Sorry!
Don't worry about it.

那不是你们班的本子，是我们班的本子。
对不起。
没关系。

These aren't your class' notebooks. They're ours.
Sorry!
Don't worry about it.

这是谁的笔？是你的笔吗？
这不是我的笔，是老师的笔。

Whose pen is this? Is it yours?
It's not my pen. It's the teacher's.

张红：这是你的课本吗？
王飞飞：这不是我的课本，我的课本
在书包里。
张红：这是谁的课本？
王飞飞：我不知道。

Zhang Hong: Is this your textbook?
Wang Feifei: No, it's not; mine
              is in my bag.
Zhang Hong: Whose textbook is it?
Wang Feifei: I don't know.

词汇表
Vocabulary

A

阿姨	āyí	aunt	6

B

爸爸	bàba	father	6
班	bān	class	8
棒	bàng	great	2
本子	běnzi	notebook	8
鼻子	bízi	nose	*5
笔	bǐ	pen	8
菠萝	bōluó	pineapple	3
不	bù	no, not	8

C

长	cháng	long	5
橙子	chéngzi	orange	*3
尺子	chǐzi	ruler	*8
草莓	cǎoméi	strawberry	3
聪明	cōngming	smart	*2

D

大	dà	big	5
大象	dàxiàng	elephant	4
的	de	possessive particle	5
弟弟	dìdi	younger brother	6

*表示只要求认知，不要求掌握的词。 It (*) refers to the words which students are required to recognize, not to use

电脑	diànnǎo	computer	7
电视	diànshì	TV set	*7
动物	dòngwu	animal	4
对不起	duìbuqǐ	sorry	8

E

| 耳朵 | ěrduo | ear | *5 |

G

钢笔	gāngbǐ	fountain pen	*8
高	gāo	high	5
哥哥	gēge	older brother	6
个	gè	(measure word for both people and objects)	3
个子	gèzi	stature	5
狗	gǒu	dog	4

H

| 好 | hǎo | nice, good | 2 |
| 很 | hěn | very | 5 |

J

脚	jiǎo	foot	*5
叫	jiào	be called	1
姐姐	jiějie	older sister	6

K

看	kàn	look	7
可爱	kě'ài	cute	*2
课本	kèběn	textbook	8
酷	kù	cool	*2

L

老师	lǎoshī	teacher	*1/2
里	lǐ	in, inside	8
两	liǎng	two	3

M

妈妈	māma	mother	6
马	mǎ	horse	*4
吗	ma	a question particle	4
芒果	mángguǒ	mango	*3
猫	māo	cat	4
没关系	méiguānxi	don't worry about it	8
妹妹	mèimei	younger sister	6
名字	míngzi	name	5

N

哪儿	nǎr	where	7
那	nà	that	6
奶奶	nǎinai	grandmother	*6
呢	ne	a modal particle	3
你	nǐ	you	1
你好	nǐ hǎo	hello	1
你们	nǐmen	you (plural)	*1/2
鸟	niǎo	bird	*4
您	nín	you (in polite way)	*1/2
柠檬	níngméng	lemon	3

P

旁边	pángbiān	side	7
朋友	péngyou	friend	6
漂亮	piàoliang	pretty	2

| 苹果 | píngguǒ | apple | 3 |

Q

| 铅笔 | qiānbǐ | pencil | *8 |

R

| 人 | rén | people, person | 3 |

S

上边	shàngbian	above	7
什么	shénme	what	1
是	shì	be (am, is, are)	1
手	shǒu	hand	*5
手机	shǒujī	cell phone	7
书	shū	book	7
叔叔	shūshu	uncle	*6
书包	shūbāo	bag	8
帅	shuài	handsome	2
谁	shuí	who	6

T

他	tā	he, him	4
她	tā	she, her	4
它	tā	it	4
头发	tóufa	hair	4

W

| 我 | wǒ | I, me | 1 |

X

西瓜	xīguā	watermelon	3
喜欢	xǐhuan	like, be fond of	4
小	xiǎo	small	*5
下边	xiàbian	below	7
香蕉	xiāngjiāo	banana	3
橡皮	xiàngpí	eraser	*8
谢谢	xièxie	thanks	2
姓	xìng	family name	1
熊猫	xióngmāo	panda	*4
学生	xuésheng	student	*1/6

Y

眼睛	yǎnjing	eye	5
爷爷	yéye	grandfather	*6
也	yě	also, either	4
椅子	yǐzi	chair	7
柚子	yòuzi	grapefruit	*3
右边	yòubian	right	7
鱼	yú	fish	4
圆珠笔	yuánzhūbǐ	ball-point pen	*8

Z

再见	zàijiàn	goodbye	1
在	zài	be in/at/on	7
这	zhè	this	6
真	zhēn	very; really	2
知道	zhīdào	know	8
桌子	zhuōzi	table	7
足球	zúqiú	football	7
嘴	zuǐ	mouth	5
左边	zuǒbian	left	*7

郑 重 声 明

图书在版编目（CIP）数据

体验汉语初中学生用书 . 第 1 册 / 国际语言研究与发展
中心 . —北京：高等教育出版社，2008.6（2009重印）
ISBN 978-7-04-022272-2

Ⅰ . 体 ⋯　Ⅱ . 国 ⋯　Ⅲ . 汉语－对外汉语教学－教村
Ⅳ . H195.4

中国版本图书馆 CIP 数据核字（2008）第 075022 号

策划编辑　徐群森　　**责任编辑**　鞠　慧　　**责任印制**　朱学忠

出版发行	高等教育出版社		**购书热线**	010 - 58581350
社　　址	北京市西城区德外大街 4 号		**免费咨询**	800 - 810 - 0598
邮政编码	100120		**网　　址**	http://www.chinesexp.com.cn
总　　机	010 - 58581000			http://www.hep.com.cn
			网上订购	http://www.chinesexp.com.cn
经　　销	蓝色畅想图书发行有限公司			http://www.landraco.com
印　　刷	北京佳信达欣艺术印刷有限公司		**畅想教育**	http://www.widedu.com
开　　本	889 × 1194　1/16			
印　　张	6.5			
字　　数	182 000		**版　　次**	2008 年 6 月第 1 版
插　　页	2		**印　　次**	2009 年 4 月第 2 次印刷

物 料 号　22272-00